Do What You Love

Fragility of Your Flame

Poems, Photography and Flash Fiction

M J MALLON

mjmallon.com

Cover Design by: Colleen Chesebro

Photography: All photography except cover design by the author

DEDICATION

To my mum and dad, my daughters, hubby, my family and friends you are so dear to my heart.

CONTENTS

THE FATES

This short book of poems is a snapshot of various heartfelt periods of my life, a nostalgic looking back giving an insight into who I am and who I hope to be.

I've applied artistic licence interpreting the three sisters of fate, the Morai: Clotho, Lachesis and Atropos as being jovial and friendly creatures, who share a discussion with me, a mere mortal, about my life to date. I reckon, being friends with the three goddesses of fate is an exceptionally good idea!

The usual interpretation of the fates is harsh, with the eldest fate Atropos choosing the manner of death, by cutting the threads of an individual's life with her dreaded shears. Often the fates are described as old and ugly in literature, whereas in the medium of art, a more becoming interpretation is often taken.

Clotho is known as the spinner, spinning the threads of life on her spindle. Lachesis, the alloter, measures the length of life with her measuring rod and Atropos (the inflexible,) ends it all with a snip, snip of her ruthless shears – when your time is up, it is up!

The three, either together or individually, are often pictured weaving or binding thread, or are seen reading or writing the book of fate.

Sometimes, the Fates may be associated with a specific time period, in this case, Atropos is associated with the past, Clotho the present, and Lachesis the future.

I've taken this meaning and assigned the fates to specific time periods in the format of this collection. This is a personal celebration of family, the places I have lived and intend to live in, the friendships and hopes I have for the future.

And... the overarching theme is to do what you love.

I hope that the three goddesses of fate will approve!

ACKNOWLEDGEMENTS

To the writing, poetry and blogging community I owe you so much. Particular thanks to Colleen Chesebro for her continued enthusiasm, encouragement and kindness, inspiring me to write poetry and for including my poetry in her books: Word Weaving #1, a word craft journal of syllable verse: The Moons of Autumn, A Wordcraft Journal of Verse.

And to Robbie Cheadle and Kaye Lynn Booth for publishing my poetry in the anthology Poetry Treasures 2 Relationships - Wordcrafter Poetry Anthology.

To the wondrous Sisters Of The Fey: Colleen Chesebro, Adele Marie Park, Debby Gies (D G Kaye,) Sally Cronin and Annette Aben thank you for your help and to all my beta readers and supporters in the writing community you are wonderful: Colleen, Adele, Debby, Sally, Richard Dee and Ritu Bhathal.

FRAGILITY OF YOUR FLAME

hibiscus flower

fragility of your flame

memories not lost

recalled by rain drops falling

caressing tender petals

With a snip of her shears Atropos handed me the pick of the bunch, the largest eye-catching flame red, hibiscus flower. She smiled and gestured for me to come closer.

"Child, your life's journey has begun," she said.

I giggled, not comprehending what Atropos meant. I was only five. A child, whose only cares were to play, dance and sing.

"The steps you take will decide where you will go, who you will meet, and what your life will be," said, Lachesis, with a serious expression.

"Remember each step is as important as the last. Each step must not be taken lightly for each will take you to the next, and the next," said Clotho, as she continued to spin the threads of life.

Atropos returned many years later whilst I was sitting on a rock surrounded by a forest upon a hill, in Scotland, in my childhood home, Blackhall.

She told me that she wished to see if childhood still resided within my heart.

I smiled.

"Your childhood flame burns brightly. It took you many years of soul searching to discover your true self."

I turned to her, "Yes that is true. For many years, I couldn't comprehend who I truly was meant to be. I was sometimes happy but sometimes discontented. Until now."

"I am so proud of you," Atropos said, "But, sad for those whose paths are thwarted. Your husband's creativity was thwarted, this saddens me. Does he still play?"

"He still plays, Atropos. His guitar still sings."

"I am glad. His father meant well," said Atropos.

"I know. His father wanted the best for him. He wanted him to have a secure job, to live a stable and safe life. He was too young to travel the world in a rock band."

"Sometimes you must gamble a little to embrace what you love. But yes, his father meant well. I wonder what would have happened if he had gone? Would he have become a rock star?" said Atropos curiously, with a twinkle in her eyes.

"I wonder that often I do, Atropos. And the consequences of which. Perhaps we would never have met.

"It is his fate to meet and to have his two dear daughters with you," said Atropos "Your stars are aligned to be together."

"Yes, but so much could have stood in your way. As a child you were faraway in Hong Kong, if you hadn't returned to the UK, you would never have met him," said Atropos.

"Yes, that is true. And my father brought us together, reuniting after a split up when we were young, before we were married."

"As I said, it is meant to be," Atropo smiled. "When you return to your childhood home what thoughts cross your mind?"

"I am always so happy to return, Atropos, as it is my second home, my much-loved home from home. I miss it so much, the festivals, the lights, the shadows, everything."

MY HOME FROM HOME – EDINBURGH

It calls me

this Scottish City

beautiful

lights twinkle

Edinburgh's dark shadows

perfect time and place

your buildings

adorned like parcels

pink in blue

they twinkle

my home from home forever

the best gift of all

I see you

bright castle hiding

beyond trees

magic night

such a blue sky highlights you

nestled on a hill

TOURIST ATTRACTION

make up check hat check,

time to beguile the tourists,

hunt the illusion,

where my legs should be there's air.

find my pins when punters gone!

(Note: pins is a slang word for legs.)

SCULPTURE FACE

-

an enchanting face,

sculpture that sees, smiles and lives,

art's favourite place,

closed nostrils don't breathe the grass,

air spells curiosity...

Image: Joan Miró – Personnage (Person)

Scottish National Gallery of Modern Art Belford Road (Modern One) Edinburgh.

When I met Atropos again I was in my back garden in Cambridge looking at old photos. She joined me, and as we turned the page to a photo of myself and my dear mother she lifted my hat off my head. "You love art galleries and funny sculptures! And that bonny knitted hat suits you. I like this photo of you and your mum very much. Your mother has great character, I see it in the way she stands."

"Yes," I replied. "Her past shaped her too. During the Japanese occupation of Malaysia, she lived through such terrible times. Her mother disappeared, leaving her in the care of distant relatives – her father wasn't a fit man. It's not surprising that my mother snatched at freedom for a time, climbing trees, and my father…"

"He became an adventurer too. All those years travelling abroad in exotic locations: Papua New Guinea, The Far East, Africa, The Middle East, Fiji, so many stamps in his passport! He has never lost that spirit of adventure. Indeed. I believe he sang in Russian, (which he learnt during his national service,) at his ninety first birthday party. Charmed the waitress, didn't he? What a delight!"

We sat in companionable silence for a moment.

"Your bond is deep, that is good. Sadly, not everyone has that special relationship with their parents. You are blessed," said Atropos.

I placed my favourite old hat on her head.

"For you," I said smiling, warmed by her kind words.

"Thank you, but no. The hat is you. We mustn't confuse life's true path and progression by accepting gifts. We must keep life simple. Enjoy your hat. I'm glad that you enjoyed your special day out with your mum and your birthday celebration with your dad."

ME AND MUM

me and mum

posing together

two gals out

shopping trip

but much more – mother daughter

friends, always best friends.

DAD'S THE BEST

Dad,

is great,

from his birth,

one of a kind,

he likes a challenge,

a dapper gentleman,

whose impeccable taste shines,

I'd describe him to impress you,

just like his grandfather before him,

he dazzles all those he meets with his charm.

***

from the beginning

he was so adventurous,

Now ninety he sings,

Russian songs to our waitress,

for the record – he's handsome!

Atropos met me by the pier in Brighton, her expression full of joy. "Natasha has done so well. Both Natasha and Georgina bring you such light. They are so different in many ways, but both have kindness and such strength of character in their heart."

"Yes," I replied, my heart beating with happiness.

"Till we meet again, Enjoy this wondrous day. The sun is shining. I won't keep you. Enjoy your daughters! The fashionista, Georgina studied in Manchester for a time, and Natasha... Brighton was her home for a while.''

GRADUATION BRIGHTON

calm and wild like life

the sea stretches beyond sight

opportunity glimmers in faraway shores

reach beyond your wildest dreams

FASHIONISTA!

an aspiration, to study

seek adventure

a huge opportunity,

scary too, fashionista!

transform, my little diva.

OUR JEWEL WAS LOST

our jewel was lost

playing hiding just chilling

we couldn't find her

until she turned up

joker!

this house hides people I swear.

OUR SOCKS ARE LOST

our socks are lost,

the washing machine claims them,

perhaps it eats them,

until one turns up - hurrah!

this house hides cute socks I swear.

Atropos hugged me close, catching a drop of my tears on her finger. "Natasha will come back," she said, soothingly.

"I know, but she is so far away. South Korea, it is the other side of the world!"

***

"You cried for a full day. It saddened me to see your tears, but it is her path to take." said Atropos.

In the background, I could hear the whispers of Lachesis saying:
"This decision will enrich her life, you'll see. She will do magnificent things, but you must let her go, so in time she can return,"

I nodded and sighed. "I know."

GONE FOR A YEAR - MISSING YOU!

The riptide hid in two shallow foreign suitcases. Tee-shirts lay crushed against jumpers, jeans pressed unfolded next to sandals and boots.

I lifted the larger suitcase up it was heavy but not as heavy as my pounding heart.

No traffic impeded our journey. The ripples began early, too early. We shared coffee but nothing to eat. The departure gate beckoned. The riptide began. It burst out of me. I cried, no I wailed. Guilt crashed against waves of sadness. Sadness wrestled and drowned my heart. Never again will I feel such depths of emotion. My adventurer, daughter had gone.

I knew that Atropos would come to soothe my pain. So much had happened. My girls were grown now. I was in the garden planting seeds when she arrived.

"I'm sorry," she said. "We all suffer in small, or big ways in our lives. It is a part of who we become. It brings resilience and compassion for all other living beings."

"Yes," I replied. "That is true. They are both strong. They will weather their storms. I am so proud of them."

She nodded, and said, "And so you should be."

MY DAUGHTERS

Two young girls, one blonde one dark, my girls,

My daughters, grown now. I remember

Trips, sunshine, parks, castles,

Ball parks, parties, giggles,

Sleepovers.

Oh, the sleepovers! Crazy friends, fights, bullies,

Shenanigans, strange confessions.

It was simpler then!

How life changes.

Until hormones raging,

Enter the boyfriends. Staying over!

Not, if dad has his way. Ever. They plead.

Determined. He weakens, gives in.

I do too, not knowing

What to do.

Starts off well, until tears, heartbreak,

A hug, a kiss. Mr. Blue Eyes

is not so carefree I say, but girls

in love don't listen.

Who would?

Don't trust a player, I cry. Do they take

My advice? Sometimes not enough.

They ask friends, me, everyone,

Make choices.

I sigh.

Now the drama's nearly over. I tremble.

Expecting the next crisis to come

rippling around the lake.

The waters swaying. It's stiller now.

They're wiser.

I'm ecstatic! They've escaped their troubles

They've put up their moats. Hurrah.

Don't cry my beauties.

You did the right thing

The waters yelling.

Nasty slaps, stares, cheats, assorted

Vicious nasties, hooded hoodlums

And gangs don't make a man

But kindness does, you'll see.

Find your soulmate

For your own dear castle. Rejoice

my lovelies you've learnt

To be brave and true.

I'm so proud

Of you.

Two girls, older now, both blonde,

Both lighter, my girls, my daughters

Such a sweet reflection

My dearest castle,

My family.

"Who is this handsome and splendid fellow?"
Atropos said, chuckling.

"His name is Zog," I replied.

"What a lovely dog. I see he was nervous to begin
with but now he follows you everywhere!"

"Yes, even into the shower room!"

"You can't keep him you know," said Atropos sadly.

"I know, he's not mine. He's a friend's dog come for
the day."

"Abandoned, more like," said Atropos, tut tutting.
"So, the human males can go off to the pub!"

"Yes, the devils! Poor Zog, he's shaking with fear.
I'm going to take him for a walk later to calm him."

"Oh, good idea. Have fun," said Atropos. "I think
you'll find he won't be too forgiving of his master.
You will be his special person today. Dogs have
hearts too."

ZOG THE GENTLEMAN DOG

Zog spiced up the day

warming our hearts with his charm

he sugared our attention

making friends, leaving presents,

such a gentleman dog, Zog.

The tulip field was enormous, so bright and cheerful. Atropos picked up a tulip which she had just cut with her shears. She gave it to me.

"Montreal, what an adventure!" she cried.

"I know, it was our second adventure of this kind.

Years ago, my daughters and I went to Malaysia with my mother to visit relatives.''

"How exciting! What a time you must have had. No relatives here in Montreal?''

"No, but everyone is so friendly.''

"The other day we were in a long queue at a popular restaurant called Arthurs and a lovely Canadian lady chatted to us. It made the time whizz by. Afterwards, we had the most amazing lunch. Montreal is a gastronomic delight! And you know how much I love my food!''

"And what of the botanical gardens?''

"They are immense, we arrived late and sadly only managed to see these beautiful tulips.''

"It was your fate to see their magnificence,'' Atropos replied.

MONTREAL – FIELDS OF BRIGHT TULIPS

with every dawn

inspiration finds a way

to bloom in choice words

until exhausted I dream

fields of bright tulips

Atropos touched the bark of the paperbark tree. "It peels," she said.

"Yes, isn't it a wonder!"

"It is indeed. You love the trees; I see it in your eyes. How this love has grown!"

"As a child I lived by a forest, but I didn't think much about the trees then, I was too busy playing or trudging through the woods with my brother to find our missing cat, Chester, who was always disappearing on some grand adventure. Now that I'm older I recognise and value their beauty."

"You are wise," Atropos said. "You spent a lot of time here in these botanical gardens."

"Yes, I do. I love the gardens."

"The trees are magical, and you are becoming more certain and grounded too. Stay with me awhile, let us enjoy these magnificent trees together."

PAPERBARK TREE (Etheree)

Image: Botanical Gardens Cambridge, UK

I

see you

paperbark

peeling brown curls

enticing me quick!

imagination twirls...

revealing bookish delight!

such captivating, living art

small tree, so unique, fresh and renewed

you've captured my heart, Magic Maple Bark!

DARLING AUTUMN TREE (1) – ETHEREE –

Image: Botanical Gardens Cambridge, UK

tree,

darling,

sweet beauty,

transfixed am I,

bright rich orange leaves,

surrounding you – autumn,

mighty miracle magic,

thrilling feather-light touch of leaves,

I breathe in your enchantment deeply,

lingering in your botanic kingdom.

DARLING AUTUMN TREE (2)

– REVERSED ETHEREE

Image: Botanical Gardens Cambridge, UK

I walk amongst your crisp leaves marvelling,

but time calls me – I must leave too soon,

touching bark, quickening heartbeat,

I steal a leaf feel aflame,

my feet begin moving,

but my heart stays here,

in paradise,

crowned autumn,

darling,

tree.

AN ARCHWAY OF TREES

Image: Botanical Gardens Cambridge, UK

an archway of trees

in this bright winter garden

red-coated lady

***

who is she?

I would like to know

her secret

***

perhaps

she will say

one day.

"Where did you happen upon this beautiful pathway?" asked Atropos.

"It was in the winter garden section of the Cambridge botanical gardens. In the distance, I saw this intriguing lady with a very bright red coat! It appears as if she's reading a book, but I can't remember what she was doing. It inspired me to write a haiga which is a syllabic observational form of poetry.

Later, on another occasion, I read an inscription on a park bench. I knew I would write a poem about it. It touched my heart.

"Yes, I knew it would," replied Atropos.

"I know what Clotho would say... *your marriage continues for many years. You were very young when you first met your husband.*"

"And yes it is true, I was eighteen... We said we would just be friends! But he walked miles to be with me in the bitter cold Scottish weather, a sure sign that we would become more than friends! One time he ended up in the back of a truck with chickens for company after hitching a lift home. We lived in the same city, but our backgrounds were many miles apart. That didn't stop us from falling in love."

My words summoned Clotho, who joined us chuckling. "Long lasting marriages must be friends and be prepared to accept the good times with the bad and make some sacrifices too. Passion is of the utmost importance too!"

"Yes, you know you love someone when you kiss them. His kisses always taste so honey sweet."

ETERNAL LOVE

It's tranquil today,

November rain, June sunshine,

seasons talk of love,

strolling side by side – mists, gusts,

welly boots squelching the earth.

Inspired by a park bench in the Botanical Gardens
Cambridge, UK

"And what is this?" asked Atropos.

"A flash fiction piece I wrote a while ago about our
world. Our precious earth."

A NEW HARVEST

Mimi knelt on the soil, her bare knees were muddy, her eyes wet with tears. Before her was one tiny shoot. Nothing moved - no creature, no human - alone she remained. The earthquake had done its worst. Her hands encircled the milk bottle of water, half full. She placed healing stones around the shoot in a circle. Her precious crystals, calming rose quartz, cradle of humankind to heal mother earth, flint to stabilise, amethyst for hopelessness and red jasper for isolation. She cried, her tears mingling with the water, the shoot twitched, and the promise of a new harvest began.

Lachesis appeared before us, disturbed by my words. "We must care for our sweet earth. If we do not… I fear for us all." She shivered and we were silent for a moment in deepest contemplation about the future of our planet.

TASTY MORSEL

shall I start eating?

this cheeky dessert mouthful,

or just admire it?

fork poised in the air trembling.

such decisions, decisions!

I picked up my fork.

"And that... what decadence is that! Ooh, I am disappointed you didn't save me a piece of that magnificent dessert," said Atropos, creasing her nose, anger colouring her cheeks. "Are you trying to rile me?"

"I'm sorry, Atropos. Please forgive me, it was so tiny, a mere tasty mouthful and it was gone!

"Yes, I saw you gobble it up! Wicked girl."

"And what is that?" Atropos asked, poking at my bulging tummy.

"A few pounds of cake," I replied.

"Huh, serves you right. But go easy! I do know how you love your food."

"Do you believe in magic?" asked Atropos.

"Stop teasing me, Fate. You know I do. Magic is in everything I do."

"Ghosts? Strange paranormal happenings?"

"Yes!"

"Fairies?"

"I have never seen a fairy. I know some who have. I wish I could."

"There is still much time for a fairy to come, perhaps, in the future," said Lachesis, pulling up a chair she sat beside us.

Atropho nodded and turned to me. "The robin, and the dragonfly came to you and inspired you to write your fictional character Mr. Sagittarius."

"Open your eyes, be patient, and a fairy will greet you soon," said Lachesis.

FAIRIES AND MAGIC

such magical eyes

fairies sit in her iris

her lashes flutter

delicate wings tickling

teasing her awake in dreams!

FAIRIES AND THE OLD LADY

on each fairy's head,

a magic crown is shining,

silver hair awaits them,

each strand a fairy's sweet home

her human heart is at peace.

THE SEA

"Where to now?" asks Atropos, her gaze is steady, her eyes kind. "I know you love the sea and yet you have not mentioned it. Why is that — mysterious girl!"

I have an old photo album in my lap, the Caribbean photos bring back memories from a time long ago when my dad used to work abroad.

I find an old piece of writing tucked in the album, its paper is crumpled, a forgotten piece I wrote at one of many writing workshops. I pass it to Atropho, and she reads, embellishing the unedited sentences to write it anew as is her way.

I revisit the pier. It is a long walk, and the Caribbean sun is scorching my back, but I do not complain. The sun is no stranger to me, or to you.

I am alone with my thoughts, thinking of you, dad.

I remember how we fished together you and I in Tortola, The British Virgin Islands. It was such a long time ago; we caught a puffer fish. How angry it had seemed. I had no idea how venomous it was. All I could see was its angry roundness, its spiky response to our human need to champion a prize catch. In haste, we threw the ball of fury back in the ocean like it was an engorged demon wriggling on the end of a hook.

Today, I cast a line forward travelling in time to another place. I know where it will land. The rocks of Bethesda Bay in Barbados – a memory akin to a mermaid rising to the surface, calling for my immediate attention. I long to revel in the complete wonder of that day when I first saw the dark, mesmerising starkness of the rock's silken beauty. How startling the rock formations had seemed highlighted against such a tranquil backdrop of golden sand. I was a carefree adult then, holidaying with my husband, laughing barefoot in the sun.

Today, I imagine I'm a child playing on those rocks again. I'm wearing a bright tomato red dress, open-toed sandals, my face is tanned ripe with the promise of future adventures. My hair is longer than it is now and the band holding it together has split apart, allowing my hair to fly free. I stop for a moment and point to the ocean. My pointed fingertip is an exclamation of sheer delight.

I return my gaze to Atropos and put down the old photo album. "Sometimes in quiet moments I listen, Atropos, hoping to hear the welcome sound of distant steel bands. I clutch at memories of people, moments shared, barbeques and carnivals in the sun. Days with my daughters and parents in Scotland building sandcastles and eating picnics by the sea. I love the sea, whether in full sunshine or biting cold days, in mirror still tranquillity and raging tempestuous fury. It is a part of me like those magnificent rocks in Bethesda Bay."

"Yes, the sea is in your soul," said Atropos.

Clotho joins us, she is studying me; her face a delightful picture of curiosity. "And what have you got planned to do next my dear girl?"

"Hubby and I are off on an adventure Clotho, before it is too late!"

I already know, but tell me again, she grinned. "Where to? The Caribbean?"

"Not to the Caribbean but yes to the sea! Of course, to the sea," I replied beaming.

"Of course!" said Atropos.

Clotho nodded. "Where to sea girl?"

"Portugal, a beautiful, charming spot called Tavira."

I opened my camera and showed Clotho my soon to be new home-from-home, enchanting Tavira, a fairy tale floating across three bridges upon a river.

I recited this poem to her...

TAVIRA

a fairy tale sight,

three bridges cross the river,

tranquil Tavira,

magic me to new delights,

a ferry to the beaches!

I turned to Atropos, but she had gone. I willed her to come back again – remembering that nostalgia for the past is never more than a heartbeat away.

"I love your poem. Will you write more about it?" Lachesis asked, leaning forward she touched my shoulder gently, her eyes shining.

"I will, I promise. You will hear all about it."

She smiled.

"I'm excited for the present, looking forward to the future but I will miss old friends. I must embrace new ones, and... keep the old..." I said, as my eyes sought them all out.

Lachesis, Clotho and Atropos smiled, their eyes shone with understanding.

OLD FRIENDS PLAY WITH BUBBLES

bubbles in the sun

playing a musical dance

basking in our sweet friendship

admiring her art

we both praise

a special day for Catherine

STRETHAM POETRY WITH FRIENDS

field of vast yellow

friends brought together through time

walking, smiling, hugs

so many reminiscences

reunite in soul's sunshine

***

a tree can tell tales

in its bark it speaks volumes

the green leaves know it

so they hug its trunk dearly

growing lush in its knowledge

***

I see a wonder

trees submerged in deep water

soaking up their roots

drinking in life's wilful woes

sorrow is an endless pit

***

will I or won't I?

my reflection says do it

I dive in and go

playful day on the river

looking for new duck friends

Atropos turned to me, "Ah, that line: looking for new duck friends! Love it."

We sat together in my parent's front garden in

blissful contemplation. She pointed to the cherry blossom on their tree, and I smiled saying:

pink blossoms on trees

childhood memories evoked

garden cherry trees

"Farewell but not goodbye Atropos! Until we meet again. The past is always in my heart but it is time to embrace my present, Clotho and my future, Lachesis."

Atropos shed a tear as she departed, "Until we reminisce again, I am never out of reach, dear old friend."

Clotho hugged me close, "Come join me. What shall we do today? Where shall we go? The present day can take you wherever you wish to be... Edinburgh, Cambridge, Manchester, Glasgow, Portugal,... "

Lachesis waved and said, "See you shortly. I know you are going to explore many new places, some you have never been before. I can't wait to be by your side. Wherever you go, whatever you do, remember to… always do what you love!"

float along with me

create clouds of sweetest joy

to do what you love

hold fate's hand as we venture

near and far on life's journey

REVIEWS

It is my dearest hope that you have enjoyed this poetry, flash fiction and photography collection. If so, please do leave a review on sites such as Amazon, Goodreads, Bookbub, etc. Reviews mean so much to authors.

They don't have to be long... just a few words would do.

Many thanks in anticipation.

ALSO BY M J MALLON

Next Chapter Publishing

YA Fantasy series, The Curse of Time

For details of publications please visit:

https://www.nextchapter.pub/authors/mj-mallon

Kyrosmagica Publishing

Poetry and Flash Fiction: The Hedge Witch and The Musical Poet

https://bookstoread/u/mv1oev

Poetry, Prose and Photography: Mr. Sagittarius
http://mybook.to/MrSagittarius

Pandemic Poetry: Lockdown Innit Poems About Absurdity

http://mybook.to/Lockdown Innit

Pandemic Anthology: This Is Lockdown

http://mybook.to/Thisislockdown

Available on Amazon kindle, Kindle unlimited and paperback

Short Stories in Anthologies:

Bestselling horror compilations

Nightmareland *compiled by Dan Alatorre*

"Scrabble Boy" (Short Story)

Spellbound *compiled by Dan Alatorre*

"The Twisted Sisters" (Short Story)

Wings of Fire *compiled by Dan Alatorre*

"The Great Pottoo" (Short Story)

Ghostly Rites 2019 *compiled by Claire Plaisted"Dexter's Creepy Caverns" (Short Story)*

Ghostly Rites 2020 *compiled by Claire Plaisted*

"No. 1 Coven Lane" (Short Story)

For all my publications and contributions to anthologies please refer to my Author Blog: https://mjmallon.com *and my Amazon Author Page:* https://www.amazon.co.uk/M-J-Mallon/e/B074CGNK4L/

ABOUT M J MALLON

MJ's favourite genres to write are Fantasy YA, Paranormal, Ghost and Horror Stories, poetry and flash fiction. She celebrates the spiritual realm, her love of nature and photography and all things bookish, magical, mystical, and mysterious at her blog home: https://mjmallon.com.

M J Mallon was born in Lion city Singapore, a passionate Scorpio with the Chinese Zodiac sign of a lucky rabbit. She spent her early childhood in Hong Kong. During her teen years, she returned to her father's childhood home, Edinburgh where she spent many happy years, entertained and enthralled by her parents' vivid stories of living and working abroad. Perhaps it was during these formative years that her love of storytelling began bolstered by these vivid raconteurs. She counts herself lucky to have travelled to many far-flung destinations and this early wanderlust has fuelled her present desire to emigrate abroad to Portugal. Until that wondrous moment, it's rumoured that she sometimes lives in Scotland and oftentimes in Portugal. Her two enchanting daughters have flown the nest but often return with a cheery smile to greet her.

She believes that life should be sprinkled with a liberal dash of extraordinarily imaginative magic! Her motto is to always do what you love, and stay true to your heart's desires!

www.ingramcontent.com/pod-product-compliance
Lightning Source LLC
Chambersburg PA
CBHW041025170626
46815CB00001B/3